NEVER FORGET

SEPTEMBER 11 AND TERRORISM IN AMERICA

Virginia Loh-Hagan

45TH PARALLEL PRESS

Published in the United States of America by Cherry Lake Publishing
Ann Arbor, Michigan
www.cherrylakepublishing.com

Reading Adviser: Beth Walker Gambro, MS, Ed., Reading Consultant, Yorkville, IL
Cover Designer: Felicia Macheske

Photo Credits: © robert paul van beets/Shuttetstock.com, cover, 1; © Gorodenkoff/Shutterstock.com, 5; © archna nautival/Shutterstock.com, 6; © Anthony Correia/Shutterstock.com, 11, 12; © Courtesy of the Library of Congress, LC-DIG-ppmsca-02137, 17; © Courtesy of the Library of Congress, LC-DIG-ppmsca-02153, 19; © Carolina K. Smith MD/Shutterstock.com, 21; © Courtesy of the Library of Congress, LC-DIG-ppmsca-01813, 22; © Courtesy of the Library of Congress, LC-DIG-ppmsca-01934, 25; © Courtesy of the Library of Congress, LC-DIG-highsm-52109, 29

Graphic Elements Throughout: © Chipmunk131/Shutterstock.com; © Nowik Sylwia/Shutterstock.com; © Andrey_Popov/Shutterstock.com; © NadzeyaShanchuk/Shutterstock.com; © KathyGold/Shutterstock.com; © Black creator/Shutterstock.com; © Edvard Molnar/Shutterstock.com; © Elenadesign/Shutterstock.com; © estherpoon/Shutterstock.com

45th Parallel Press is an imprint of Cherry Lake Publishing.

Library of Congress Cataloging-in-Publication Data
Names: Loh-Hagan, Virginia, author.
Title: Never forget : September 11 and terrorism in America / by Virginia Loh-Hagan.
Description: Ann Arbor, Michigan : Cherry Lake Publishing, 2022. | Series: Behind the curtain
Identifiers: LCCN 2021037478 | ISBN 9781534199477 (hardcover) | ISBN 9781668900611 (paperback) | ISBN 9781668902059 (pdf) | ISBN 9781668906378 (ebook)
Subjects: LCSH: September 11 Terrorist Attacks, 2001—Juvenile literature. | Terrorism—United States—Juvenile literature.
Classification: LCC HV6432.7 .L647 2022 | DDC 363.3250973931—dc23
LC record available at https://lccn.loc.gov/2021037478

Cherry Lake Publishing would like to acknowledge the work of the Partnership for 21st Century Learning, a Network of Battelle for Kids. Please visit *http://www.battelleforkids.org/networks/p21* for more information.

Printed in the United States of America
Corporate Graphics

A Note on Dramatic Retellings

Participating in Readers Theater, or dramatic retellings, can greatly improve reading skills, especially fluency. The books in the **BEHIND THE CURTAIN** series give readers opportunities to learn about important historical events in a fun and engaging way. These books serve as a bridge to more complex texts. All the characters and stories have been fictionalized. To learn more, check out the Perspectives Library series and the Modern Perspectives series, as **BEHIND THE CURTAIN** books are aligned to these stories.

TABLE of CONTENTS

HiSTORiCAL
BACKGROUND

On September 11, 2001, militants attacked the United States. These militants were al-Qaeda members. Al-Qaeda is a terrorist group. They have an extreme view of the religion of Islam. They wanted the United States to stay out of their affairs. Their leader was Osama bin Laden. Bin Laden set up a base in Afghanistan. He ordered an attack.

Nineteen al-Qaeda members hijacked 4 U.S. planes. They used the planes as missiles. Two planes were flown into the Twin Towers of the World Trade Center. These towers stood in New York City. A third plane hit the Pentagon. The Pentagon is the headquarters of the U.S. Department of Defense. It is in Washington, D.C.

FLASH FACT!

Afghanistan is in the middle of Central Asia, India, and the Middle East. It has been and continues to be invaded.

Vocabulary

militants (MIH-luh-tuhnts) soldiers who use extreme methods for a cause

terrorist (TEHR-uhr-ist) using violence for a cause

hijacked (HYE-jakd) unlawfully took over

FLASH FACT!

President Joe Biden agreed to withdraw combat troops from Afghanistan by August 31, 2021.

The fourth plane never made its target. Passengers fought the hijackers. The plane crashed in a field in Pennsylvania. Some experts think the plane was headed to the White House or U.S. Capitol.

These crashes are known as the 9/11 terrorist attacks. About 3,000 people were killed. Thousands more people were injured. It was the deadliest domestic terrorist attack on modern American soil.

The United States responded. The government sent troops to Afghanistan. They destroyed al-Qaeda's bases. They killed bin Laden in 2011. The government set up the Department of Homeland Security. This department works to stop terrorism.

CAST of CHARACTERS

NARRATOR: person who helps tells the story

KATHY: an emergency medical worker

JEFF: a New York City Police Department police officer

MARCUS: a New York City Fire Department firefighter

PRESIDENT GEORGE W. BUSH: 43rd President of the United States

KEVIN: a White student in New York City; a bully

AMNA: a **Muslim** American student in New York City

DEV: a **Desi** American student in New York City

JEREMY: a White student in New York City; Jeff's son

SPOTLIGHT
AMPLIFICATION OF AN ACTIVIST

Many people got sick from the 9/11 attacks. The explosion and dust caused many lung problems. The World Trade Center Health Program (WTCHP) was created. It paid the health care costs for some victims. The Victim Compensation Fund gave payments to those who suffered. The fund was due to run out in 2020. Activists fought to extend it for 70 more years. Luis Alvarez was one of the activists. He worked for the New York Police Department. He was one of the first responders at Ground Zero. He breathed in poisons. He got lung cancer. In 2019, he went to Washington, D.C. He spoke in front of Congress. He said, "You all said you would never forget. It is my goal and it is my legacy to see that you do the right thing for all 9/11 responders." He died several days later. The fund was extended.

Vocabulary
Muslim (MUHZ-luhm) a person who practices Islam

Desi (DEH-see) a person of South Asian, Indian, Pakistani, or Bangladeshi descent

FLASH FACT!
The Patriot Act was passed 6 weeks after the 9/11 attacks. This law allows the government to collect and share data.

NARRATOR: *It's September 11, 2001. Terrorists flew planes into the twin towers.* **Skyscrapers** *collapsed. People got trapped. Many died.* **First responders** *go to Ground Zero. This is the area in New York City where the World Trade Center fell.* **KATHY,** *an emergency medical worker, meets at the scene with* **JEFF,** *a New York City police officer, and* **MARCUS,** *a New York City Fire Department firefighter.*

KATHY: Thank you for coming here. This is a critical time. We need as many **volunteers** as possible. We need to find survivors. We need to clear this area.

JEFF: Of course. We were trained for this. We want to do our part.

NARRATOR: *The air is filled with thick smoke. Dust and* **debris** *are floating around everywhere. It's hard to see the sun. Big fires are still burning.*

KATHY: Make sure you cover your mouth and eyes. The air isn't safe. Some first responders were sent home. They got really sick.

Vocabulary

skyscrapers (SKY-skray-puhrz) tall buildings with many floors

first responders (FUHRST rih-SPAHN-duhrz) community helpers like police officers and firefighters who train to assist in emergencies

volunteers (vah-luh-TIHRZ) people who donate their time to help a cause

debris (duh-BREE) scattered pieces of waste or remains

FLASH FACT!

First responders wear masks to keep safe from poisons in the air.

JEFF: It's not just the air. Look at all this wreckage. There are sharp pieces all around us.

MARCUS: It's hard to believe the Twin Towers once stood here. Now, it's just piles of **rubble**. Some of these piles are 90 feet (27 meters) tall.

KATHY: That's why we call this area "The Pile."

JEFF: These piles are not safe. They look really unstable. They could fall at any minute.

KATHY: You're right. That's why we can't bring any trucks here. We're afraid trucks will shift the piles. This would put any survivors in danger.

MARCUS: We have to be really careful.

KATHY: That reminds me. This is dangerous work. You should write your names and phone numbers on your arms.

JEFF: Why do we need to do that?

Vocabulary
rubble (RUH-buhl) broken fragments

FLASH FACT!
Aircraft hijackings are rare today.

KATHY: Just in case. You could get crushed or fall into one of the **voids**. People need to be able to identify you.

MARCUS: What are voids?

KATHY: They're air pockets. They're everywhere among the piles.

JEFF: People might not have been able to escape the falling buildings. They may be trapped in the voids.

NARRATOR: *A cry sounds in the distance.*

MARCUS: Did you hear that? I heard a cry for help.

KATHY: Let's check the voids. There might be survivors there. People may be trapped alive in the rubble.

MARCUS: We don't want to cause more damage. We can use our bare hands. We can dig out the rubble.

SPOTLIGHT
A SPECIAL EFFECT

A tree was found at Ground Zero a month after the 9/11 attacks. The tree was a Callery pear tree. It was damaged. The New York City Department of Parks and Recreation took care of it. They nursed it back to life. In 2010, the tree was replanted at the 9/11 memorial site. It is now known as the "Survivor Tree." It blooms every spring. In 2013, the Survivor Tree Seedling Program was launched. Each year, seedlings from the Survivor Tree are given to communities that have faced tragedies. For example, seedlings were sent to Parkland, Florida. This is where a gunman killed 17 people at Marjory Stoneman Douglas High School. Each community promises to care for the tree. The Survivor Tree and its seedlings remind people of the power of healing.

Vocabulary
voids (VOYDZ) gaps or holes

FLASH FACT!

After Ground Zero was cleaned out, it was called "the pit." Today, 3 skyscrapers, a museum, and a memorial stand there.

JEFF: That'll take too long. Let's try filling small buckets with debris. Then we can pass the buckets to each other. We can move the rubble and clear this area.

KATHY: That sounds like a great idea.

NARRATOR: *First responders worked all day and all night. They rescued people. They recovered human remains. They cleaned up the area and made it safe. Marcus, Jeff, and Kathy are taking a break. They're listening to the radio, where* **PRESIDENT GEORGE W. BUSH** *is giving a speech.*

MARCUS: Turn up the radio. President Bush is speaking.

PRESIDENT GEORGE W. BUSH: Today, our fellow citizens, our way of life, our very freedom came under attack in a series of **deliberate** and deadly terrorist acts.

JEFF: I still can't believe this happened. How could people do this?

MARCUS: Terrorists are **extremists**. They use violence to scare people.

PRESIDENT GEORGE W. BUSH: These acts of mass murder were intended to frighten our nation into **chaos** and retreat. But they have failed. Our country is strong. Terrorist attacks can shake the **foundations** of our biggest buildings. But they cannot touch the foundation of America.

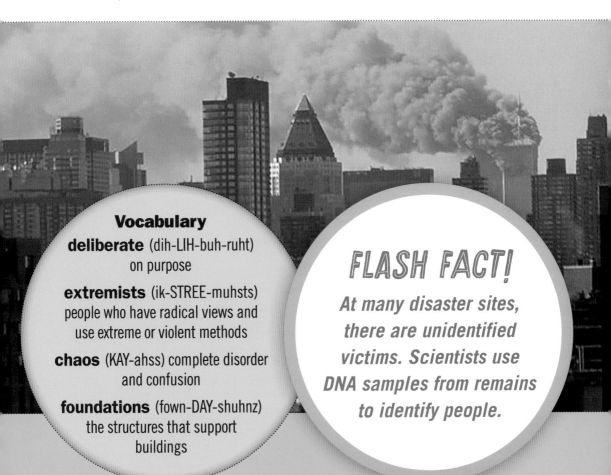

Vocabulary

deliberate (dih-LIH-buh-ruht) on purpose

extremists (ik-STREE-muhsts) people who have radical views and use extreme or violent methods

chaos (KAY-ahss) complete disorder and confusion

foundations (fown-DAY-shuhnz) the structures that support buildings

FLASH FACT!

At many disaster sites, there are unidentified victims. Scientists use DNA samples from remains to identify people.

JEFF: Why would they attack us?

PRESIDENT GEORGE W. BUSH: America was targeted for attack because we're the brightest **beacon** for freedom and opportunity in the world.

MARCUS: If they can take down the United States, then they win. But like Bush said, we're too strong.

PRESIDENT GEORGE W. BUSH: Today, our nation saw evil— the very worst of human nature. And we responded with the best of America.

KATHY: We're part of the best of America. Think about how many people showed up today. We risked our lives. We helped each other.

PRESIDENT GEORGE W. BUSH: This is a day when all Americans from every walk of life unite in our resolve for justice and peace. None of us will ever forget this day.

MARCUS: I'll never forget.

JEFF: I won't either.

KATHY: United we stand.

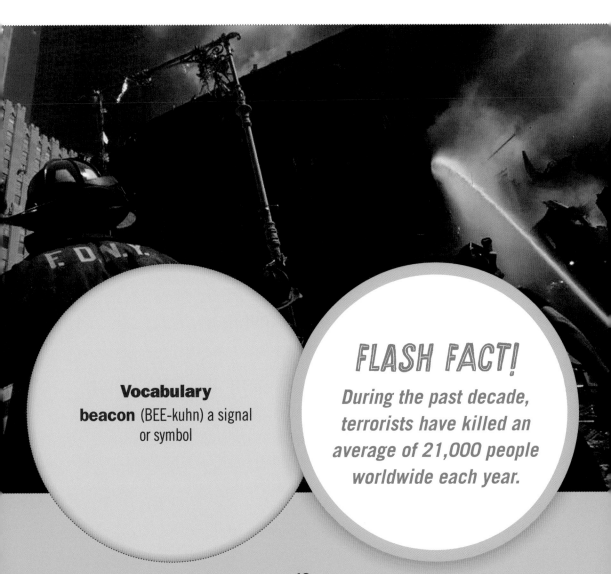

Vocabulary
beacon (BEE-kuhn) a signal or symbol

FLASH FACT!

During the past decade, terrorists have killed an average of 21,000 people worldwide each year.

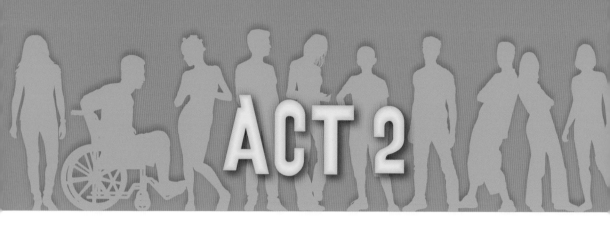

ACT 2

NARRATOR: *About a month has passed since the 9/11 attacks.* KEVIN, AMNA, DEV, *and* JEREMY *are students. They go to a school in New York City. They are eating lunch in the cafeteria.*

KEVIN: Hey, al-Qaeda!

AMNA: My name is Amna. I'm not al-Qaeda.

KEVIN: You're wearing that turban.

AMNA: It's a **hijab**. It's part of my religion.

KEVIN: It was your religion that blew up the Twin Towers.

AMNA: That is not what happened. Remember what President Bush said: "The face of terror is not the true faith of Islam. That's not what Islam is about. Islam is peace. These terrorists don't represent peace. They represent evil and war."

DEV: Millions of people follow Islam. Al-Qaeda is a small **sect**. They're extremists. They do not represent Muslim people. It's racist to assume all Muslim people are terrorists.

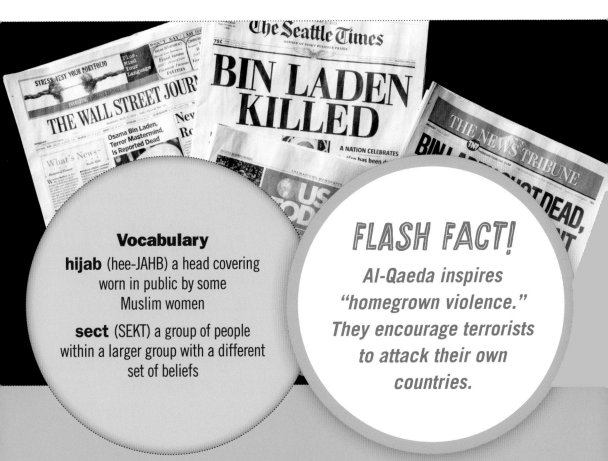

Vocabulary

hijab (hee-JAHB) a head covering worn in public by some Muslim women

sect (SEKT) a group of people within a larger group with a different set of beliefs

FLASH FACT!

Al-Qaeda inspires "homegrown violence." They encourage terrorists to attack their own countries.

KEVIN: Well, you should know. You're Muslim too.

DEV: Actually, I'm not. I'm Desi American.

KEVIN: What does that mean?

Vocabulary
cowardly (COW-uhrd-lee) not brave

FLASH FACT!
Domestic terrorists tend to attack immigrants and people of color. Racism plays a role in terrorism.

DEV: My family emigrated from India.

KEVIN: India. Iraq. It's all the same.

DEV: That's a racist comment. If you get a map, you'll see they're in different parts of the world.

KEVIN: Well, maybe you both should go back to where you came from.

AMNA: We're from here. We were born here. Just like you.

KEVIN: You are not like me. Remember what President Bush said: "Make no mistake. The United States will hunt down and punish those responsible for these **cowardly** attacks."

JEREMY: The president meant terrorists. We can't blame all Muslims for something a small group did. That would be wrong.

DEV: I wish you didn't see us as your enemies. We're Americans.

JEREMY: The president also said Muslims should be treated with respect.

KEVIN: Why are you on their side? You should be mad like me. Your dad died at Ground Zero.

AMNA: He did? I'm sorry to hear that.

JEREMY: His name was Jeff. He was a police officer. He was a first responder. He died while looking for survivors. He did that out of love. He wouldn't want me to hate.

Vocabulary
harassed (huh-RAHST)
bothered or attacked

FLASH FACT!

Religious terrorism has killed the largest number of people.

24

AMNA: We have lost so much because of 9/11.

DEV: We have all suffered.

KEVIN: How have you suffered?

DEV: My aunt was **harassed** in the street. She was beat up. She was just walking home from donating blood for the survivors.

KEVIN: Why did she get beat up?

DEV: People thought she was al-Qaeda. Like you, they blamed all people who looked Muslim for 9/11.

JEREMY: Amna, how have you suffered?

AMNA: My whole family has faced **discrimination**. My cousin got fired. My aunt's business lost customers. My brother got kicked off the football team. People threw rocks at our **mosque**'s windows. I don't feel safe anymore.

KEVIN: I didn't know any of this. I'm so sorry for what I said to both of you.

DEV: Why did you say those things?

KEVIN: I hear my parents saying things. I hear people in the news saying things. I'm just so angry about what happened. I took it out on you.

AMNA: Everyone is angry. Everyone is scared. Something terrible happened to all of us.

About 13,238 Americans were born on September 11, 2001. They're known as the "9/11 Babies." This group's worldview has been shaped by the 9/11 attacks. Jayna is a 9/11 baby. She was born at 6:00 p.m. in Washington State. She said, "A big part of why I wanted to be a nursing major has to do with being born on 9/11 and wanting to give back and live up to the legacy of those that gave their life on that day." There's another group. About 100 babies were born soon after their fathers died on 9/11. They're called the "Children of 9/11." Lauren McIntyre's father was a police officer. He ran into one of the towers to rescue people. He died doing so. McIntyre said, "I could only imagine how much courage someone could have to go into a situation like that. He didn't have to go in. He did anyway. It's beyond amazing."

Vocabulary

discrimination
(dih-skrih-muh-NAY-shuhn)
the unjust or unfair treatment of
different categories of people

mosque (MAHSK) a Muslim
place of worship

FLASH FACT!

There are more news reports about terrorism than actual terrorist attacks.

JEREMY: After my dad died, my mom and I were **devastated**. We felt so lost.

KEVIN: What did you do?

JEREMY: We wanted to make sense of everything. We learned more about al-Qaeda.

DEV: What did you learn?

JEREMY: Osama bin Laden told his followers to attack anyone who didn't agree with their version of Islam. He called Americans **infidels**.

AMNA: He said killing enemies was holy work. He told his soldiers that they'd be heroes. He promised they'd be rewarded in the next life.

KEVIN: Why did people listen to him?

DEV: This happens all the time. We have so many examples in history. Think about Adolf Hitler. In World War II, his hate led to the **Holocaust**. More than 6 million Jewish people were killed.

AMNA: We can't repeat the mistakes of our past. We can never forget.

DEV: We need to fight for justice. We must unite against hate.

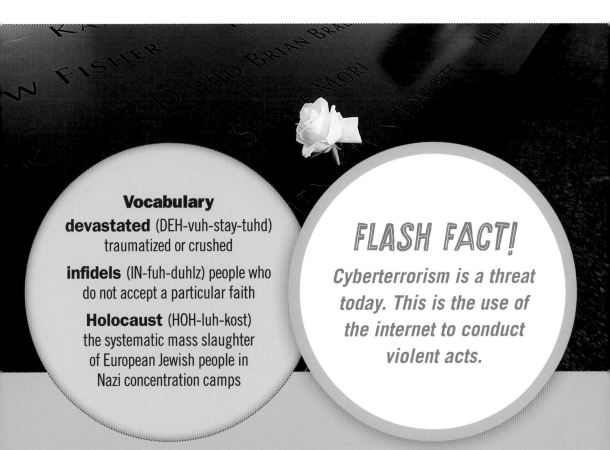

Vocabulary

devastated (DEH-vuh-stay-tuhd) traumatized or crushed

infidels (IN-fuh-duhlz) people who do not accept a particular faith

Holocaust (HOH-luh-kost) the systematic mass slaughter of European Jewish people in Nazi concentration camps

FLASH FACT!

Cyberterrorism is a threat today. This is the use of the internet to conduct violent acts.

FLASH FORWARD
CURRENT CONNECTIONS

The 9/11 attacks happened in 2001. But their legacy lives on. We are still feelings its effects. There is still so much work for us to do.

- **Fight against Islamophobia and anti-Asian hate:** Islamophobia is the fear or hatred of Muslims. There's been an increase in hate crimes against Muslims, Arabs, Middle Eastern people, and South Asians. These groups were falsely blamed for 9/11. Hate against them is based on how they look. Extreme terrorists are at fault, not Islam. Islam is a peaceful religion. Today, those with Asian backgrounds are being blamed for COVID-19. They have been attacked and harassed. It's important to not fear or hate others.

- **Say no to violence:** ISIS is the Islamic State of Iraq and Syria. They are a Sunni jihadist group. They are extreme. They want to create an Islamic state. They were inspired by al-Qaeda. Many violent terrorist attacks are linked to them. They use social media to recruit and promote. Some ISIS leaders have claimed COVID-19 is punishment for disobeying Islam. They're using the pandemic to recruit members. Avoid groups that use violence as a tool. It's important to be critical about everything you read.

- **Address domestic terrorism:** Terrorists are not just foreigners. They can be U.S. citizens. White supremacist and far-right nationalist groups are also threats to homeland security. On January 6, 2021, rioters attacked the U.S. Capitol. The Capitol is the meeting place for Congress. There was a violent riot. At least 5 people died. More than 140 were hurt. It's important to protect our democracy.

CONSIDER THIS!

TAKE A POSITION! Since the 9/11 attacks, travel bans have been enacted in an attempt to protect national security. Learn more about these bans. Do you agree or disagree? Argue your point with reasons and evidence.

SAY WHAT? Social media spreads information. It also connects people. Explain the role social media plays in terrorism. Explain how social media can stop terrorism.

THINK ABOUT IT! People of color, especially immigrants, are often blamed for problems in the United States. Who was blamed for the September 11 terrorism? What other groups have been blamed for things? Why are some people considered scapegoats? Scapegoats are people or groups who get blamed for the faults of others.

Learn More

Maranville, Amy. *The 9/11 Terrorist Attacks: A Day That Changed America.* Mankato, MN: Capstone Press, 2021.

Orr, Tamra B. *September 11 and Terrorism in America.* Ann Arbor, MI: Cherry Lake Publishing, 2018.

Rusick, Jessica. *September 11, 2001: Then and Now.* Minneapolis, MN: Abdo Publishing, 2020.

Tarshis, Lauren, and Corey Egbert. *I Survived the Attacks of September 11, 2001.* New York, NY: Scholastic, 2021.

INDEX

ABOUT THE AUTHOR

Dr. Virginia Loh-Hagan is an author, former K–8 teacher, curriculum designer, and university professor. She's currently the director of the Asian Pacific Islander Desi American (APIDA) Center at San Diego State University. She remembers where she was on September 11. She was driving to her job teaching third grade in Chula Vista, California. She lives in San Diego with her one very tall husband and two very naughty dogs.